Learning to Read, Step by Step!

Ready to Read   Preschool–Kindergarten
• big type and easy words • rhyme and rhythm • picture clues
For children who know the alphabet and are eager to begin reading.

Reading with Help   Preschool–Grade 1
• basic vocabulary • short sentences • simple stories
For children who recognize familiar words and sound out new words with help.

Reading on Your Own   Grades 1–3
• engaging characters • easy-to-follow plots • popular topics
For children who are ready to read on their own.

Reading Paragraphs   Grades 2–3
• challenging vocabulary • short paragraphs • exciting stories
For newly independent readers who read simple sentences with confidence.

Ready for Chapters   Grades 2–4
• chapters • longer paragraphs • full-color art
For children who want to take the plunge into chapter books but still like colorful pictures.

STEP INTO READING® is designed to give every child a successful reading experience. The grade levels are only guides; children will progress through the steps at their own speed, developing confidence in their reading. The F&P Text Level on the back cover serves as another tool to help you choose the right book for your child.

Remember, a lifetime love of reading starts with a single step!

To my mother
—S.A.K.

Cover photograph credits: Kareem Abdul-Jabbar (Allsport); Michael Jordan (John Biever/ *Sports Illustrated*); LeBron James (AP Photo/Alex Menendez); Larry Bird (Richard Mackson/ *Sports Illustrated*); Kevin Durant (some rights reserved by Josh Kouri, found on Flickr Creative Commons).

Text photograph credits: pp. 1 & 3: see cover photograph credits, above; p. 4: Rick Stewart/ Allsport; p. 6: Walter Iooss, Jr.; p. 11: Sheedy & Long/*Sports Illustrated*; p. 18: Allsport; p. 24: Jerry Wachter/Focus on Sports; pp. 30, 43 & 44: Focus on Sports; pp. 36 & 47: some rights reserved by Keith Allison, found on Flickr Creative Commons; pp. 45 & 46: WDPG share.

Visit us on the Web!
StepIntoReading.com
randomhousekids.com

Educators and librarians, for a variety of teaching tools, visit us at RHTeachersLibrarians.com

Library of Congress Cataloging-in-Publication Data
Kramer, Sydelle.
Basketball's greatest players / by S.A. Kramer.
pages cm. — (Step into reading, step 5)
ISBN 978-0-553-53394-1 (trade) — ISBN 978-0-553-53395-8 (ebook)
1. Basketball players—United States—Biography—Juvenile literature. 2. Basketball players— Rating of—United States—Juvenile literature. I. Title.
GV884.A1K727 2015 796.3230922—dc23 [B] 2014044625

Printed in the United States of America   10 9 8 7 6 5 4 3

This book has been officially leveled by using the F&P Text Level Gradient™ Leveling System.

BASKETBALL'S GREATEST PLAYERS

by S. A. Kramer

Random House 🏠 New York

Introduction

What's the hottest sport around? Basketball. It's 48 minutes of nonstop action. Take your eyes off the court for an instant and you'll miss a slam dunk, a behind-the-back pass, or a sneaky steal.

Basketball is the only sport completely developed in America. A Massachusetts teacher, Dr. James Naismith, invented the game with his wife's help in 1891.

Today, people shoot hoops all over the world. From college campuses to NBA (National Basketball Association) arenas, basketball keeps fans on the edge of their seats.

And nobody plays it better than the men of the NBA. Fans love to argue about who's the greatest. This book tells you all you want to know about the best players ever.

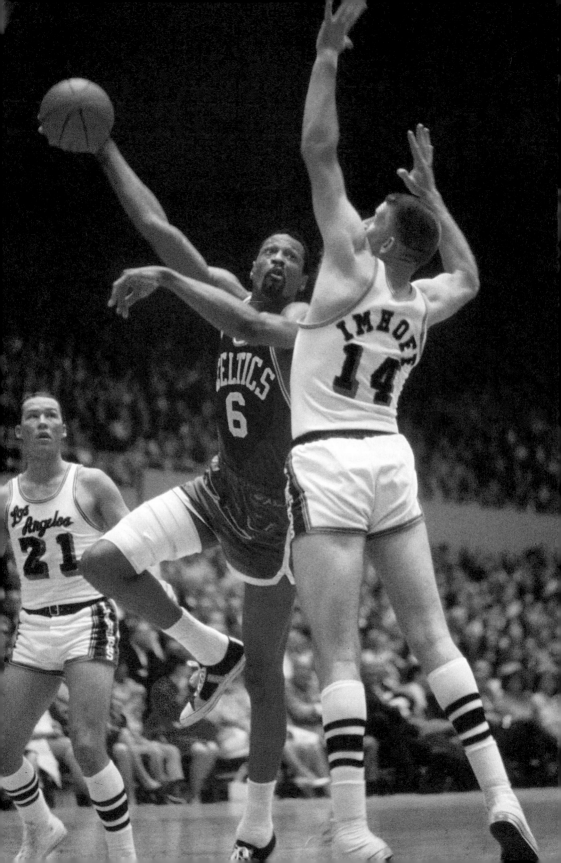

1
DEFENSE!

College ball, 1953. The game between the University of San Francisco and Brigham Young University has just started. Bill Russell, a sophomore (second-year student), is San Francisco's center. At 6'10", he can outjump everyone on the floor.

The man Bill's guarding dribbles around him. When the man goes in for an easy layup, San Francisco's captain scowls at Bill. "Why don't you try playing some defense?" he hisses.

Bill gets angry. He knows the captain doesn't like him because he's black. He decides he'll show the guy exactly what defense is. So he sticks to his man as though his life were at stake. The player doesn't score another point.

It's then that Bill realizes that defense can

win games. From now on, he vows, that's what he'll concentrate on.

Other centers feel defense is unimportant. If they don't have the ball, they just stand around the basket. When they block shots, they slap the ball hard into the stands.

Bill shows them a new way of playing. He makes defense lead to fast breaks and scoring. Timing his leaps, he tips blocked shots to teammates racing downcourt. He tears around the floor, stealing balls and grabbing rebounds.

In 1956, Bill joins the NBA as the Boston Celtics' only black player. His style single-handedly changes basketball defense.

The league is startled when Bill doesn't care about scoring. But the Celtics don't need points from him to win. They count on him to make sure the team works together. Bill becomes the greatest team player on the only team in history, in *any* sport, to win eight championships in a row.

But Bill isn't very popular. He keeps his distance from almost everybody, even refusing to sign autographs. He doesn't care if he's liked—all he wants is respect.

Bill was born poor in a small Louisiana town divided by race. Growing up, he hardly spoke to any white people.

When he was twelve, his mother died. He never got over it. But he's learned to act tough. Even in a game, he hides his true feelings. He seems calm on the court, yet he often throws up before he plays.

There's one thing Bill never hides—his pride in his race. He is one of the first black athletes to speak out against prejudice. The Celtics name him the first black head coach in professional sports. Later, he becomes the first black sportscaster on national TV. Bill is a great champion. That's why, in 1980, he was named the best basketball player ever by the Professional Basketball Writers Association of America.

WILLIAM FELTON RUSSELL

★★★★★★★★★★★★★

(RUSS, SECRETARY OF DEFENSE)

Born 2/12/34   6'10", 215 lbs.

**Played center for the Boston Celtics
1956-69
Most Valuable Player 5 times
Hall of Fame**

★★★★★★★★★★

- Second in career rebounds: 21,620
- Led the league in rebounds 4 times
- Won more championships than any other player: 11
- College team won 55 games in a row and 2 National Collegiate Athletic Association (NCAA) titles
- First player to win the MVP 3 seasons in a row
- Appeared in 12 straight All-Star Games (1958-69)
- Named best basketball player ever by the Professional Basketball Writers Association of America (1980)

2
SCORE!

Hershey, Pennsylvania. March 2, 1962. The Philadelphia Warriors and the New York Knicks are about to play one of the last games of the season.

Wilt Chamberlain, the Warriors' star center, barely notices. He's tired—he didn't get any sleep the night before. But he knows he'll do well anyway. Wilt's proud and always needs to be the best. He wraps a rubber band around his right wrist. It's his good-luck charm.

Besides, 7'1" Wilt is already the NBA's first giant superstar. Before him, centers weren't much taller than other players. They didn't weigh close to his 270 pounds. Now every team wants someone like Wilt— a huge scoring center who can take over the game. His height and strength have changed basketball forever.

Tonight Wilt is an iron man. In the first half, he scores forty-one points! He sweats so much he has to change his jersey at halftime. Then he drinks half a gallon of milk to put liquids back in his body.

In the second half, Wilt keeps piling on the points. There's no defense against his dipper dunk, a stuff through the net. No one can stop his fadeaway jumper or his finger roll.

Now the game's in the fourth quarter. The Warriors are winning, but all eyes are on Wilt. He has over eighty points. Fans are yelling—they want him to score one hundred. No one has ever done it before.

The Knicks are determined to stop Wilt. They hang all over his back. They pound him with fouls. But Wilt's teammates keep getting him the ball—and Wilt keeps scoring.

A minute to go. Wilt has ninety-eight points. Can he make one last basket? He's exhausted—he's played the entire game. When he gets the ball, he shoots—and misses.

But wait! A teammate grabs the rebound. He passes it to Wilt. Wilt slips by the defense and goes in for a layup. *Swoosh!* He's scored a hundred points in one game, an NBA record that has never been broken.

Fans rush the court. Wilt escapes to the locker room and sits quietly on a bench. He can't quite believe what he's done. He's made thirty-six baskets and twenty-eight free throws—and also pulled in twenty-five rebounds.

Fans aren't surprised. Wilt's been a great athlete since he was a teenager. By age fourteen, he was seven feet tall! His huge size made him perfect for many sports.

But he hated his long, skinny body. Wherever he went, he'd try to sit down so people wouldn't stare at him. Basketball made him feel better about his size.

Wilt was fast. He could jump fifty inches straight up in the air. His hands were so big that one coach said he handled the ball "like you or I would a grapefruit." To build up his strength, he worked out with five-hundred-pound weights.

A great college player at the University

of Kansas, Wilt joined the NBA in 1959. Back then, most players were white. Wilt was black—and the biggest player of all. So every move he made was studied by fans and experts alike. Wilt, a proud man who needed to be the best, felt pressure to win right away.

Between 1960 and 1973, Wilt nearly ruled the game. He led the league in rebounds eleven times and was the top scorer seven years in a row. In 1,045 games, he never once fouled out.

And yet his team won the championship only twice. Sportswriters and fans blamed Wilt. Unlike his rival, Bill Russell, he was not a team player—he hogged the ball.

But as he grew older, Wilt changed his game. He took fewer shots and made more of them. He passed to the teammate most likely to score. In 1968, he became the only center ever to lead the league in assists.

That year he was traded to the Lakers,

and soon learned to play strong defense. In 1971–72, he led them to a thirty-three-game winning streak—and the championship. "Where there's a Wilt," he always said, "there's a way."

In 1999, he died suddenly at the age of sixty-three. But fans will always remember "Wilt the Stilt," one of basketball's greatest.

WILTON NORMAN CHAMBERLAIN

★★★★★★★★★★★★★

(WILT THE STILT, THE BIG DIPPER)

Born 8/21/36   7'1", 270 lbs.

**Played center for the Philadelphia (later Golden State)
Warriors, Philadelphia 76ers, and Los Angeles Lakers,
1959-73
Most Valuable Player 4 times
Hall of Fame**

★★★★★★★★★★

- First in career rebounds: 23,924
- Most rebounds in a single game: 55
- Most rebounds in a single season: 2,149
- Most points scored in a single game: 100
- Most points scored in a single season: 4,029
- Most complete games in a single season: 79
- Highest career rebound average: 22.9 per game
- Highest scoring average in a single season: 50.4
- Highest field goal percentage in a single season: .727
- Fifth in career points: 31,419
- Second in career scoring average: 30.1
- Most points in a rookie season: 2,707
- Most assists by a center in a single game: 21
- League's leading scorer most times: 7
- Most baskets without a miss in a single game: 18
- Most baskets in a row without a miss: 35
- Appeared in 13 All-Star Games (1960-69, 1971-73)

3
SKYHOOK

May 10, 1974. The sixth game of the NBA finals. Fans in the Boston Garden are going wild. Their Celtics are beating the Milwaukee Bucks, 101–100, in double overtime. Just seven seconds are left in the game.

The Bucks have the ball. It's their last chance to score. Their star center, Kareem Abdul-Jabbar, grabs a pass from the sidelines. There's no time to waste.

Kareem tries to get the ball to his teammates. But they're closely guarded. He has to take the shot himself!

The 7'2" giant dribbles once, then turns. Three seconds left. Fans are screaming, players scramble around him—but he feels as if he's completely alone.

With his back to the basket, Kareem leaps

into the air. He raises the ball high above his head with his right arm, and balances it on his fingertips.

Then, with a flick of his hand, he guides the ball toward the hoop. It's his famous skyhook! Kareem first made this shot in college because he wasn't allowed to dunk—he scored too many points. Whenever he shoots the skyhook, he's as graceful as a dolphin.

The ball drops through the basket! The net doesn't even move. Two points! The Bucks win, 102–101. Kareem lifts his arms in triumph. Always great in the clutch, he's won another one for his team. Later, he says he felt "all power was mine."

Kareem's been a basketball sensation for years. He was the talk of the game by the time he reached eighth grade. His skinny body and long arms seemed meant for the sport. The taller he grew, the better he got. He was seven feet tall by age fourteen.

But young Kareem hated being famous. He was quiet and shy, a serious student who loved music and books. His greatest wish was to be the same height as his friends.

Being famous, Kareem said later, "pushed me inside myself." He learned to hide his feelings on and off the court. That could make him look relaxed, as if he didn't care. Fans complained he didn't play hard.

Were they wrong! Kareem scored and scored everywhere he played. His college team, UCLA, lost only two games in three years. In the NBA, he led the Bucks to one championship and the LA Lakers to five.

No one could keep Kareem away from the hoop. Season after season, he was a leader in scoring and rebounding. A six-time MVP, he scored more points than anyone else in basketball.

For most of his career, Kareem was the tallest man in the game. When opponents tried to guard him, they could never reach over him. Going for the ball, they often accidentally scratched his eyes, so Kareem had to wear goggles.

Despite his size, Kareem never pushed players around. He never talked trash. But he did have a temper. Once he slugged a player who elbowed him hard. He knocked the man out—and broke his own hand in the process.

Kareem was a superstar. Still, basketball could make him anxious. He'd have trouble sleeping and get severe headaches called migraines. To calm himself before a game, he'd read a newspaper or a book.

And he took comfort from his religion. Born Catholic, he became a Muslim in college. He dropped his old name, Lew Alcindor, and chose a new one—Kareem Abdul-Jabbar. The name means "noble, generous servant of the powerful God"— a worthy name to take with him into the record books as basketball's greatest scorer.

KAREEM ABDUL-JABBAR

★★★★★★★★★★★★★★

(LEW, CAP, MURDOCK)
(BORN FERDINAND LEWIS ALCINDOR, JR.)

Born 4/16/47   7'2", 225 lbs.

**Played center for the Milwaukee Bucks
and Los Angeles Lakers, 1969-89
Most Valuable Player 6 times
Hall of Fame**

★★★★★★★★★★

- First in career points: 38,387
- Third in blocked shots: 3,189
- Second in games played: 1,560
- First in minutes played: 57,446
- First in field goals scored: 15,837
- One of only 3 players in the 30,000/10,000/5,000 Club—at least 30,000 points, 10,000 rebounds, and 5,000 assists
- Fourth in career rebounds: 17,440
- First in personal fouls: 4,657
- Scored 1,000 or more points in 19 seasons
- Appeared in 19 All-Star Games (1970-77, 1979-89)

4
THE LEADER

January 18, 1986. Larry Bird storms into the locker room. His Boston Celtics are playing badly. It's halftime, and they're losing to the Atlanta Hawks by twenty-seven points. The Hawks and their fans seem to be laughing at them.

Larry knows his team is the best in the league. But they've gotten lazy. If he doesn't shake them up, they could blow their chance at the championship.

Larry grabs a chair and throws it across the room. Then he throws another, and another. Chairs are flying all over the place! Soon he's screaming, shouting insults at his teammates.

The Celtics don't argue. Larry is their leader, and they know he hates to lose.

A forward who can shoot, pass, and

rebound, he plays so unselfishly he makes them a better team. Many experts feel he's the best forward the game has ever seen.

When halftime is over, Larry leads his Celtics onto the floor. He scores basket after basket. His passing is so sharp, he always finds the open man. All over the court on defense, he anticipates the Hawks' every move.

Larry's play inspires the Celtics. Fired up, they catch the surprised Hawks and win in overtime, 125–122. Larry has sparked the victory.

When he was in high school and college, few coaches expected him to succeed in the NBA. He didn't jump well and was often the slowest man on the floor. But the coaches didn't count on Larry's determination.

Starting in high school, he carried his basketball everywhere, practicing at night, on weekends, even in the rain. At six a.m. every school day, he'd shoot free throws for an hour and a half. If he was seated, he worked on his dribbling. When he broke his ankle, he just learned to pass the ball while on crutches.

He kept practicing hard all through college. "Basketball was all I thought about, all I wanted to do," Larry said. The game made him feel good about himself even in times of trouble. When he was nineteen, his father killed himself. His mother worked such long hours, she was hardly ever home. But with a ball in his hands, Larry could set aside these problems. The game made him feel tough and in control.

Points came easy to him in college, but he knew it would be different in the NBA. So when he joined the Celtics, he always prepared carefully for a game. To warm up, he took sixty jump shots. He studied every possible move to make up for being slow. Once he took the floor, he knew where the ball was every moment.

Larry showed how good he was right from the start. In his rookie year, he helped the Celtics achieve the biggest season turnaround in NBA history. The year before, the team's record had been 29–53. With Larry, their record improved to 61–21.

Fearless on the court, Larry trash-talked, even to older stars. One player reported, "He'd say 'In your face' or 'You can't guard me'—whatever he could use to throw you off balance."

Once he'd been shy and clumsy, but now he was so confident, he knew he could make the winning shot. His passing was so accurate, he could hit a man eighty feet downcourt. While Larry was with the Celtics, the team won three NBA crowns.

In 1997, he brought his winning ways to coaching. With the Indiana Pacers, Larry was named Coach of the Year his very first season. By 2000, he had taken the team to the NBA finals. Now he's the Pacers' president, the only man in basketball ever to be voted Most Valuable Player, Coach of the Year, and Executive of the Year.

He's still a perfectionist. And he still hates to lose—even if he's only playing Ping-Pong with friends!

LARRY
JOE BIRD

★★★★★★★★★★★★★★

(HICK FROM FRENCH LICK, LARRY LEGEND)

Born 12/7/56   6'9", 220 lbs.

Played forward for the Boston Celtics, 1979-92
Most Valuable Player 3 times
Hall of Fame

★★★★★★★★★★

- Rookie of the Year (1979–80)
- Led the league in free-throw percentage 4 times
- Made 71 free throws in a row
- Led the league in 3-pointers 2 times
- One of 12 players to score over 20,000 total points, haul down over 5,000 total rebounds, and tally 5,000 total assists
- In 1985–86, finished in the top 10 in scoring, rebounding, steals, free-throw percentage, and 3-point shooting percentage—one of the greatest seasons ever
- Appeared in 12 All-Star Games (1980-88, 1990-92)

5
THE GREATEST

Michael Jordan has a dream. More than anything, he wants to make his high school basketball team. If he succeeds, he'll feel better about himself. He won't mind if kids tease him about his haircut, or the way his tongue sticks out when he shoots hoops.

Michael goes to the tryouts and does his best. Two weeks later, a list goes up. "I looked and looked for my name," he says.

It isn't there. At first Michael feels numb. But when he gets home, he says, "I went to my room and I closed the door and I cried."

Still, he doesn't give up. When summer comes, he's on the court practicing every day.

By the time school starts again, Michael is over 6'3". It's easier for him to score now. And all that practicing has taught him how the game should be played. This time, when he tries out for the team, he makes it.

Michael's a good athlete. But no one thinks he'll be a star. Most colleges don't want him to join their teams. The University of North Carolina, though, is willing to take a chance. In 1982, during his first year there, Michael erases all doubt about his talent with just one shot.

He's a skinny guard on the Tar Heels, playing in the NCAA (National Collegiate Athletic Association) championship game. With just seconds to go, the team is one point behind.

Seventeen feet from the hoop, Michael gets the ball. The championship, he realizes, is in his hands. He coolly takes a jump shot—and scores! He's won the game! His basket is nicknamed "the Shot."

Michael is an instant star. By 1984, he's playing for the NBA's Chicago Bulls. Only a rookie, he still wins the scoring crown.

No one looks as fast. No one jumps as

high. With his body strong from lifting weights, he rarely tires. His gigantic hands help him score anytime. Foul shots are easy: Michael can make them with his eyes closed.

He's a nice guy off the court, but he turns tough at the tip-off. When Michael trash-talks opponents, they usually don't talk back. No one wants to get him mad—he plays even better then.

If the Bulls need a basket, he always gets the ball. He says, "I love it when it comes down to that one moment and it's all in my hands." But he's not just an unstoppable scorer. He's also a great passer and defender.

Soon everyone in America wants to see Michael play. Fans love it when he leaps and seems to hang in the air, floating to the basket as though he'll never come down. Experts quickly recognize him as the greatest basketball player ever.

Michael leads the Bulls to three NBA titles in a row. He turns basketball into the sport that everyone wants to play. His talent and charm make him the world's most popular athlete.

But in 1993, tragedy strikes. Michael's father is murdered. He's overwhelmed with grief. Basketball doesn't seem important anymore, so he quits playing.

After a while, though, he misses the game. In 1995, he returns to the Bulls. Fans everywhere are thrilled to have him back.

And he hasn't lost a step. From 1996 to 1998, he leads Chicago to three more NBA championships. He is voted MVP for the fifth time. When he retires in 1999, he's still the best player on the court.

In 2000, Michael comes back to the sport again. He becomes part owner and president of the Washington Wizards. The next year he puts on a uniform and plays with the team. He says it's the best way to teach them how to win.

Michael's playing days finally end

in 2003. But even now, he's not out of basketball—he owns the Charlotte Hornets. And his business smarts and Jordan clothing line have helped make him the first NBA player ever to become a billionaire.

MICHAEL
JEFFREY JORDAN

★★★★★★★★★★★★★★

(MJ, AIR JORDAN, HIS AIRNESS)

Born 2/17/63   6'6", 195 lbs.

Played guard for the Chicago Bulls and Washington Wizards, 1984-93, 1995-98, and 2001-03
Most Valuable Player 5 times
Hall of Fame

★★★★★★★★★★

- First in average points per game: 30.1
- Third in steals: 2,514
- Fourth in all-time scoring: 32,292
- Won the NBA scoring title more than anyone else—10 times
- Holds the playoff-game scoring record: 63 points
- Highest playoff scoring average: 33.45 points
- Most 50-point playoff games: 8
- Most points ever in the playoffs: 5,987
- 6 NBA Finals MVP Awards
- Scored 25,000 points faster than any other player except Wilt Chamberlain
- One of only 2 players to score over 3,000 points in a season
- One of only 3 NBA players ever to block more than 100 shots and make over 200 steals in a season, and the only player to do it twice
- Appeared in 14 All-Star Games (1985-93, 1996-98, 2002-03)

6
COMING HOME

August 8, 2014. Akron, Ohio. A tall, handsome man in a black T-shirt and baseball cap walks calmly onto the field at InfoCision Stadium. Close to 25,000 screaming fans greet him. LeBron James has come home.

King James, as he's nicknamed, circles the stage, his arms raised in triumph. Suddenly a young man in a number 23 jersey—LeBron's number—jumps a police barricade. He leaps onto the stage and throws his arms around the superstar. After he's led away, LeBron takes the microphone. "I love you. I'm back," he says.

With these words, the number one basketball player in the world celebrates his return to the Cleveland Cavaliers. Ohioans couldn't be happier. Four years ago, LeBron broke their hearts when he left the Cavs for the Miami Heat.

He'd announced the move in a 2010 TV special, *The Decision*. "This is very tough," he'd explained. But his thinking was clear. The Heat gave him a real chance to "win championships," which would mark him as a truly great player.

His news rocked the sports world. In a furious Cleveland, there was fighting in the streets. Some people were so angry, they posted videos of themselves burning their number 23 jerseys.

Even the Cavs' owner was enraged. He called LeBron a "deserter" and a "coward." And in Akron, where LeBron was born, everyone felt betrayed. After all, it was there that he had gone from near-homelessness to stardom.

Life in Akron had been hard for LeBron. He wasn't sure who his father was, and his mother was "nowhere near prepared to deal with it all." She and LeBron were so poor, they drifted from home to home. Once they had to move five times in three months. The little boy was shy, lonely, and frightened. He often skipped school.

Enter Frank Walker, LeBron's peewee football coach, and his wife, Pam. The couple invited LeBron to live with them until his mother got back on her feet. He thrived under their care.

By the age of nine, LeBron had become a great athlete. Football was his first love, but basketball was where his size, quickness, and ball-handling skills mattered most. He loved the game's fast pace, teamwork, and "the adventure of putting the ball in the rim."

When he was eleven, he caught the eye of a coach for an eleven-and-under team called the Shooting Stars. On the team were three kids who would later become like brothers to LeBron. Together they called themselves the Fab Four.

The Fab Four were so close that they chose to attend high school together and play for the basketball team. LeBron was top scorer. He was so talented, college and pro scouts showed up at games to check him out.

LeBron fever spread fast. He was hounded by autograph seekers, interviewed on TV, promised multimillion-dollar contracts—and he was still just a teen! Only a handful of players had gone directly from high school to the NBA. Would LeBron be next?

In the 2003 NBA draft, he was the first pick, and the Cavaliers grabbed him. But in pre-season games, he seemed unprepared for the fast, high-powered NBA. Was he ready to be a pro? Some analysts wondered if they had overrated LeBron.

In the season's very first game, he silenced the critics, draining jumpers like a veteran and running the floor with speed and power. The Sacramento Kings beat his

Cavs, but LeBron scored twenty-five points. Some experts consider it one of the great debuts in sports history. That season LeBron was NBA Rookie of the Year.

It was the first of many achievements. By 2013, he was a four-time MVP with two championship rings and two NBA Finals MVP Awards. He has been an All-Star every year he's played except one. Now that Ohio's hero is back home with the Cavs, who knows what triumphs are to come?

LeBron James

★★★★★★★★★★★★★★★

(KING JAMES, LBJ, CHOSEN ONE, BRON-BRON)

Born 12/30/84   6'8", 240 lbs.

Played shooting guard and small forward for the Cleveland Cavaliers, 2003-10; small forward and power forward for the Miami Heat, 2010-14; and forward for the Cavaliers, 2014- Most Valuable Player 4 times

★★★★★★★★★

- First among active players in average points per game: 27.5
- First among active players in minutes played per game: 39.5
- Finished first in field goals 4 times
- Fifth among active players in assists: 5,790
- Fifth among active players in free throws: 5,382
- 2 NBA Finals MVP Awards
- 2 All-Star Game MVP Awards
- Has appeared in 10 All-Star Games so far (2005-14)
- 1 NBA scoring title (2008)
- NBA Rookie of the Year (2004)
- Named to the All-NBA First Team 8 times (2006, 2008-14)
- Named to the NBA All-Defensive First Team 5 times (2009-13)
- Cavaliers' all-time leading scorer
- Player of the Week 45 times
- Player of the Month 27 times

7
MORE GREATS

Other athletes have achieved greatness, too, changing basketball with their superb skills. Here are some of them:

Oscar Robertson ("the Big O") was the NBA's first big guard—a strong, physical player who avoided flashy moves. A great believer in the basics of the game, Oscar "killed you with fundamentals." He was so committed to perfection, he'd scream at teammates if they made a mistake. The top high school and

Oscar Robertson

college player of his time, he could pass, shoot, dribble, and rebound. Played 1960–74.

Earvin ("Magic") Johnson, Jr., was one of the most popular players in NBA history. A quick, tall guard for the Los Angeles Lakers, he brought enthusiasm, joy, and amazing talent to the game. Thrills, too, since he was able to pass the ball as if he had eyes in the back of his head.

Earvin Johnson, Jr.

He is considered the greatest point guard ever, terrific on both ends of the court—a true team player who led his team to five championships and won three MVPs.

In 1991 he made headlines when he revealed that he had the AIDS virus. Ever since, he has worked for AIDS prevention and education, and has built a business empire that brings stores and services to poor communities. In 2012, Magic became part owner of the Los Angeles Dodgers. Played 1979–91, 1996.

Kobe Bryant ("the Black Mamba") has been the Los Angeles Lakers' shooting guard since joining the team right after high school. Modeling himself on Michael Jordan, another shooting guard, he's been an All-Star sixteen times and has won five NBA championships.

Kobe Bryant

A superstar who always practices hard, he is the youngest player ever to score over 30,000 points. Kobe can be arrogant, and at times he hogs the ball. But no one wants to win more. Maybe that's why he's so clutch: in 2012, NBA coaches named him the player they most wanted taking the shot with the game on the line. Started playing in 1996.

Tim Duncan ("the Big Fundamental") is a power forward and center for the San Antonio Spurs, and he plays both offense and defense at the highest level. A five-time NBA champ and three-time Finals MVP, Tim's not flashy or emotional— but no one in the

Tim Duncan

game is more respected, or a better leader. Low-key and modest on and off the court, he's a "quiet giant," secure in his own skin.

Nearing the end of his career, he still avoids the spotlight—and still takes over games. Started playing in 1997.

A PLAYER TO KEEP YOUR EYE ON

Kevin Durant ("the Servant"), the young star forward of the Oklahoma City Thunder, just may be on his way to the Hall of Fame. Only twenty-six years old, he's already won an MVP and four scoring titles.

Kevin Durant

It's easy to see why Kevin has been called a scoring prodigy. He's quick and deadly accurate, using his amazingly long arms to shoot over smaller players and attack the rim around taller players. And he can play defense, too. Remarkably confident on the court, he's a different guy off it. Said to be "almost inhumanly humble," he's considered "the nicest guy in the NBA." Started playing in 2007.